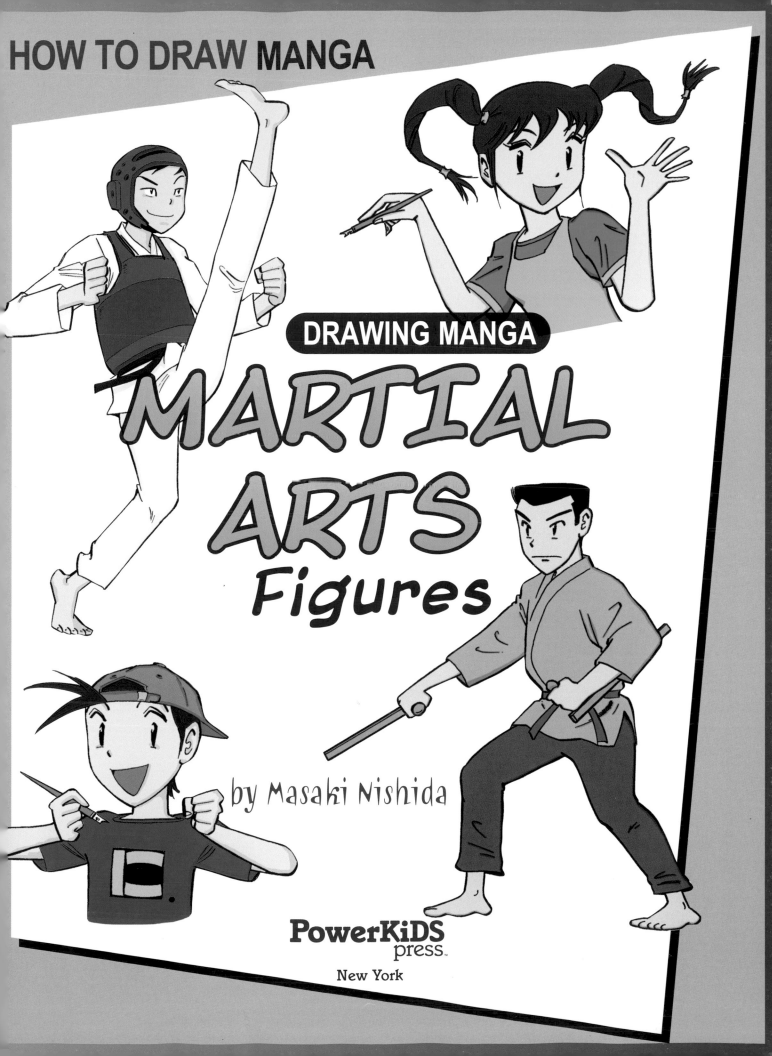

Published in 2008 by The Rosen Publishing Group, Inc.
29 East 21st Street, New York, NY 10010

First Edition

American Editor: Victoria Hunter
Japanese Editorial: Ray Productions
Book Design: Erica Clendening
Coloring: Erica Clendening, Julio Gil, Thomas Somers, Gregory Tucker

Manga: Masaki Nishida

Library of Congress Cataloging-in-Publication Data

Nishida, Masaki, 1960-
  Drawing manga martial arts figures / Masaki Nishida.   \ 1st ed.
      p. cm.   \ (How to draw manga)
  Includes index.
  ISBN-13: 978-1-4042-3850-3 (library binding)
  ISBN-10: 1-4042-3850-6 (library binding)
 1. Martial arts in art \Juvenile literature. 2. Human beings \Caricatures and cartoons \Juvenile literature. 3. Comic books, strips, etc. \Japan \Technique \Juvenile literature. 4. Cartooning \Technique \Juvenile literature. I. Title.
  NC1764.8.M38N57 2008
  741.5'1 \dc22
                              2007015191

Manufactured in the United States of America

CONTENTS

About Manga

Hi! My name is Masaki. I love reading and drawing manga and would like to introduce you to this fun and **unique** art form. Being a **creative** artist allows me to draw as well as write. It's exciting to put my art and stories together and see what I've made. I have done a **variety** of manga-style projects, from sports to history to nature!

In this book, my friend Sayomi and I will show you how to draw eight manga martial arts figures step-by-step. We will also give you some story ideas to use when you've learned to draw your figures. The possibilities are endless!

The supplies you will need to draw manga martial arts figures are:

- A **sketch** pad
- A pencil
- A pencil sharpener
- A ballpoint or a fine-felt pen
- An eraser
- Your imagination!

Manga has been very *popular* in Japan for a long time, and recently manga's popularity has spread around the globe. Manga is special because it borrows ideas from American *comic books* and European and American movies. Because of manga's pop *culture influence* it has far-reaching appeal.

People like manga because of the *combination* of pictures and *text*. The stories are fun and easy to follow for readers of any age. Anything is possible in the world of manga and that's part of the reason it is so great!

Hi! My name is Sayomi. Masaki and I are going to help you draw manga martial arts figures!

You can use the skills you acquire from this book to write your own manga stories. We hope you'll use this book as *inspiration*, to write, draw and create. Have fun *exploring* the manga martial arts world!

DRAWING AN
AIKIDO FIGURE

Fight me, Sayomi!

When practicing aikido, you can throw your **opponent** to the ground!

1 Draw an oval for the head.

2 Draw a rectangle for the body.

3 Draw a **trapezoid** for the uniform. Add small circles and rectangles for the arms and hands.

4 Repeat the previous three steps to add an opponent.

5 Add more details, and add ink to the lines you want to keep.

6 Erase extra pencil lines.

7 Color your drawing and you're done!

DRAWING A JUJITSU FIGURE

Jujitsu is a ruthless martial art! You can throw, hold, hit, and sometimes even use **weapons** against your enemy!

1. Draw an oval for the head.

2. Add a rectangle for the body.

3. Draw circles and rectangles for the arms, hands, and legs.

4. Add more details, such as the tonfa. Draw over the lines you want to keep with ink.

TONFA is an *ancient* Chinese weapon from which the modern-day police baton is derived.

5. Erase the pencil lines.

6. Color in your Jujitsu **character** and he's ready to fight.

DRAWING A
JUDO FIGURE

The main **technique** of judo is to throw or force down your enemy!

1 Draw an oval for the head.

2 Draw a rectangle for the body.

3 Draw rectangles for the arms and legs. Draw circles for the hands and feet.

4 Add facial features and the **uniform** details.

5 Ink the lines you want to keep and erase the pencil lines.

6 Add shading and color to your judo character.

DRAWING A
KARATE FIGURE

Oh no...

I love karate because I love to punch, kick, and strike!

1 Draw an oval for the head.

2 Draw a rectangle for the body.

3 Add the rest of the body using rectangles and circles.

4 Add the details to the face.

5 Keep developing your drawing and then add ink. Erase the old pencil lines.

6 Color your karate figure any way you wish.

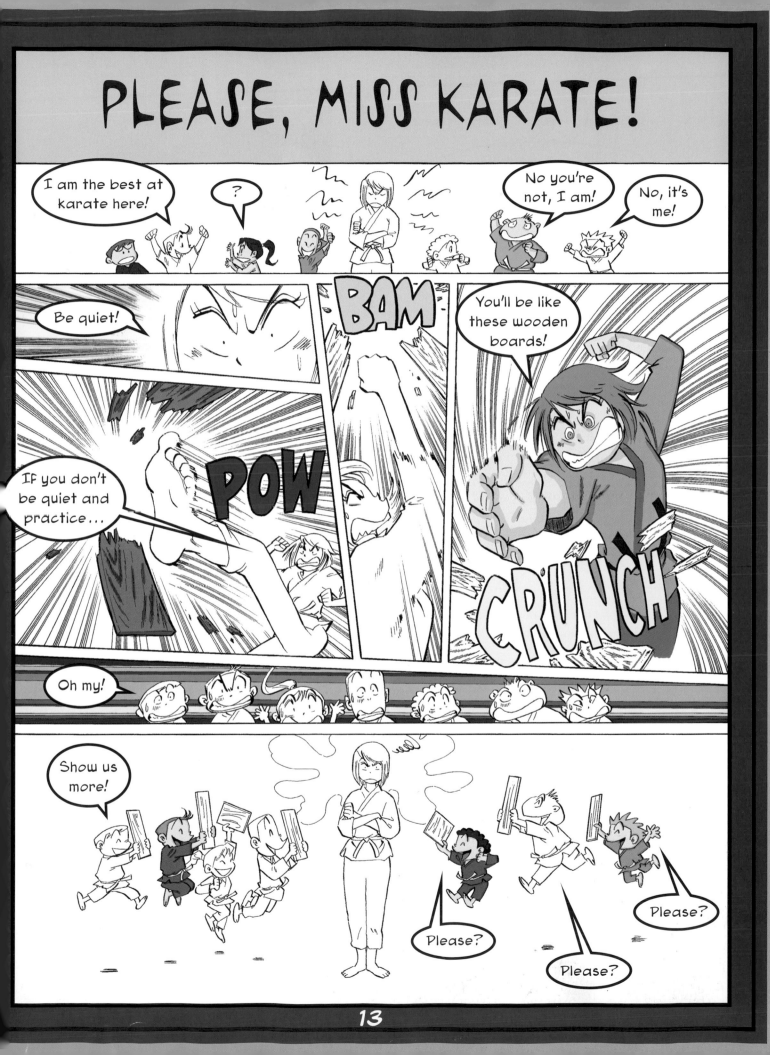

DRAWING A KUNG FU FIGURE

With its **speed** of the body and of the mind, kung fu is really cool!

1 Draw an oval for the head with a pencil.

2 Draw a rectangular shape for the body.

3 Add arms and legs with rectangles. Add hands and feet with circles.

4 Add uniform details and facial features.

5 Add ink to the lines you want to keep and erase the rest.

6 Now color in your kung fu figure. He's ready for **combat!**

ENCOURAGING KUNG FU FIGHTERS

DRAWING A
TAI CHI FIGURE

Performing tai chi involves slow movements and *elegance*. It's good for your mind and your body!

1. Draw a circle for the head.

2. Draw a rectangle for the body.

3. Add arms and legs to create the rough shape.

4. Draw more details to her face, hair, and clothing.

5. Ink the lines you want to keep and erase the rest.

6. Adding color and shading to your drawing will make it beautiful.

DRAWING A HAPKIDO FIGURE

Hapkido is a Korean martial art. Let's draw a hapkido fight!

1 Draw an oval for the head.

2 Draw a rectangle for the body.

3 Add arms and legs with small circles and rectangles.

4 Draw the opponent in the same way.

5 Add more details. Ink over the pencil lines you want to keep.

6 Erase any extra pencil lines with an eraser.

7 Add color and shading to your drawing to really bring it to life!

Uh-oh! Masaki is losing!

20

GLOSSARY

ancient (AYN-shent) Very old, from a long time ago.

character (KER-ik-tur) An individual in a story.

combat (KOM-bat) A battle or a fight.

combination (kahm-buh-NAY-shun) Things that are mixed or brought together.

comic books (KAH-mik BUHKS) Books with drawings that tell a story.

creative (kree-AY-tiv) Having different, new ideas.

culture (KUL-chur) The beliefs, practices, and arts of a group of people.

elegance (EH-lih-gunts) Showing good taste.

exploring (ek-SPLOR-ing) Going over carefully or examining.

influence (IN-floo-ents) A person or a thing that has the power to sway others.

inspiration (in-spuh-RAY-shun) Powerful, moving guidance.

opponent (uh-POH-nent) A person or a group that is against another.

performing (per-FORM-ing) Carrying out or doing.

popular (PAH-pyuh-lur) Liked by lots of people.

sketch (SKECH) A quick drawing.

speed (SPEED) How quickly something moves.

technique (tek-NEEK) A way of doing something.

text (TEKST) The words in a piece of writing.

uniform (YOO-nih-form) Special clothes worn for a job or a school.

unique (yoo-NEEK) One of a kind.

variety (vuh-RY-ih-tee) Many different kinds of things.

weapons (WEH-punz) Any objects or tools used to wound, disable, or kill.

Meet the Martial Arts Figures!

Aikido is about throws, not kicking and punching. Practitioners of aikido also wear a slightly different uniform from other martial artists.

Kung Fu is a strict physical and mental discipline, combining Eastern philosophy and fighting.

Jujitsu uses holds, throws, and blows to disable opponents. It uses the hard parts of the body, the knuckles, fists, elbows, and knees.

Tae kwon do is a modern martial art from Korea that is characterized by high, fast, and spinning kicks.

Judo is a refined version of Jujitsu. It involves throwing techniques as well as grappling, pins, control holds, and choking.

Tai chi is moving meditation and yoga combined. Movements are derived from martial arts but performed in a noncombative way.

Karate is primarily a striking art using punches, kicks, knee and elbow strikes, and open-handed techniques. It is derived from kung fu.

Hapkido is a self-defensive martial art from Korea. It uses weapons, throws, kicks, hits, and nerve pressure techniques.

INDEX